EVERYONE
DIES
YOUNG

European Perspectives:

A Series in Social Thought and Cultural Criticism

European Perspectives:
A Series in Social Thought and Cultural Criticism
LAWRENCE D. KRITZMAN, EDITOR

European Perspectives presents outstanding books by leading European thinkers. With both classic and contemporary works, the series aims to shape the major intellectual controversies of our day and to facilitate the tasks of historical understanding.

For a complete list of books in the series, see pages 97–100.

EVERYONE DIES YOUNG

Time Without Age

Marc Augé
Translated by Jody Gladding

Columbia University Press
New York

Columbia University Press
Publishers Since 1893
New York   Chichester, West Sussex
cup.columbia.edu

Originally published as *Une ethnologie de soi. Le temps sans âge*. © Editions du Seuil, 2014. *Collection La Librairie du XXIe siècle*, sous la direction de Maurice Olender.

Translation copyright © 2016 Columbia University Press

All rights reserved

Cet ouvrage a bénéficié du soutien des Programmes d'aide à la publication de l'Institut Français.

This work, published as part of a program of aid for publication, received support from the Institut Français.

Library of Congress Cataloging-in-Publication Data

Names: Augé, Marc, author.

Title: Everyone dies young : time without age / Marc Augé ; translated by Jody Gladding.

Other titles: Ethnologie de soi. English

Description: New York : Columbia University Press, [2016] | Series: European perspectives : a series in social thought and cultural criticism | "Originally published as Une ethnologie de soi : Le temps sans age, Editions du Seuil, 2014." | Includes bibliographical references and index.

Identifiers: LCCN 2015038137| ISBN 9780231175883 (cloth : alk. paper) | ISBN 9780231541596 (e-book)

Subjects: LCSH: Life cycle, Human. | Age groups. | Aging. | Self-acceptance.

Classification: LCC HM721 .A9413 2016 | DDC 305.2—dc23

LC record available at http://lccn.loc.gov/2015038137

Columbia University Press books are printed on permanent and durable acid-free paper.

This book is printed on paper with recycled content.

Printed in the United States of America

c 10 9 8 7 6 5 4 3 2

Cover design: David Drummond

References to websites (URLs) were accurate at the time of writing. Neither the author nor Columbia University Press is responsible for URLs that may have expired or changed since the manuscript was prepared.

CONTENTS

EVERYONE DIES YOUNG

THE WISDOM
OF THE CAT

We found it in the Forest of Marly, abandoned for some time, famished, imploring, and clearly determined not to let us return alone. I was of the same opinion. My parents let themselves be convinced. I was an only child. I was twelve years old. We would grow up together, the cat more quickly than me, of course.

That kitten had character and tough claws that she readily put to use, especially when I persisted in trying to teach her tricks, as though she were a circus horse. My arms were covered with wounds but suffered less than the upholstery of the living room chairs on which, to my mother's despair, she regularly sharpened her claws.

I grew up; she got older without changing much in appearance. She calmed down, I sometimes told myself a little disingenuously, knowing that I was the one who had given up provoking her. My hands and arms were no longer bloody, and our relationship became less playful, more peaceful, even contemplative. She loved to dominate the scene from the sideboard in the living room that rose just behind one of the high-backed chairs that she had massacred. When she was young, she would land on top in a single effortless bound before returning to her favorite lair with an elegant little jump. She sometimes preferred the armchair; then she would lie, precariously balanced, paws politely folded, along the edge of the chair back, watching me quietly, as though defying me to do the same. At least that was the impression this astonishing sight gave me—an impression probably stemming from my remorse as a failed animal trainer. She sought out difficulty on her own; I sometimes saw her tense her muscles, fix her gaze on the desired perch, estimate its height, and accomplish the feat via a direct floor-to-buffet flight without the intervening armchair. And then over the years, imperceptibly, her powers declined. First she gave up the buffet; then she no longer aimed for the chair back. She was happy to lie on the seat of the armchair for hours at a time, faithful to that spot but at a lower level. Eventually she had a hard time pulling herself up to the seat, which became the roof of her new retreat.

Once or twice, I tried to lend her a hand, setting her on the buffet. Without exactly taking offense at my initiative, she seemed to me disoriented and anxious to get down again as quickly as possible. This was no longer her level. I understood that I had committed a faux pas, an error of taste, or more accurately, of manners, and I was annoyed with myself. She remained even-tempered until the end, enjoying the least ray of sunshine, staying close to the radiators in winter, cocking an ear at the first cooing of pigeons when spring returned, accepting the signs of affections that we continued to lavish upon her with the same benevolent indifference that had been part of her charm since her youngest days.

Mounette (that is the name we had given her, without making any great efforts at originality) lived a long cat life and died at about the age of fifteen in my parents' apartment, which I had left a bit earlier.

Those who own domestic animals happily attribute qualities of heart and mind to them, declaring them faithful, loyal, true, and even intelligent. Besides conveying the sometimes neurotic nature of human/pet relationships, from both sides, these judgments confirm the fact that, as a general rule, the latter are not subject to the social pressures of all kinds that affect the former. Although entirely domesticated, these animals are perceived as spontaneously embodying eminently natural qualities. Do not misunderstand me; I am not suggesting here that my cat was a sage. I have not studied cat psychology. It is a question of the image that I created of her.

Later on I had two cats, a couple I really felt to be inseparable. Certainly strength of habit was the cement of their relationship, as among humans. They often squabbled when they were young, their endless games turning quickly to fights. Moreover they safeguarded their independence and happily set off alone on adventures when they lived in the country. But they quickly found each other again and lay together every evening, eyes half closed, with the air of accomplices. They grew old together, and when the first one died, the other one did not show any particular emotion, lying alone in their usual place, but he died in turn a few days later.

The cat is not a metaphor for humankind but a symbol for what could be a relationship with time that would make age an abstraction. We are awash in time, savoring a few moments of it; we project ourselves into it, reinvent it, play with it; we take our time or let it slip away: it is the raw material of our imagination. Age, on the other hand, is the detailed account of the days that pass, the one-way view of the years whose total sum when set forth can stupefy us. Age wedges each of us between a date of birth that, at least in the West, we know for certain and an expiration date that, as a general rule, we would like to defer. Time is a freedom, age a constraint. The cat, apparently, does not know this constraint.

What you will find here is neither a journal nor a memoir, even less a confession, but rather some personal remarks, beginning from my experiences and my reading. For each of us, life constitutes a long and involuntary inquiry. In this book I have tried to support a conclusion that will undoubtedly confirm some readers' intuition but will surprise others because it goes against the truisms of popular wisdom ("If youth but knew, if old age but could . . ."): as fountain of knowledge or wealth of experience, old age does not exist. To realize that old age does not exist, one only has to achieve it. Of course, the afflictions and weaknesses associated with aging are there, and very much there, more or less early, more or less dramatically, but they do not always wait for old age, and they do not strike everyone equally.

As to the state of mind and behavior of the old, they are often inferred through the language of the less old, even or especially with good intentions. In its time, the paternalistic language of the colonizers was denounced, those colonizers who were not always the most cynical but certainly the most myopic. What adjective could be found to characterize the language sometimes employed with regard to old people, who are labeled "dependents" as a sign of special attention? I am thinking of the familiarities of a few well-intentioned individuals, nurses or other medical aides for example, who readily call those they are attending "gramps" or "granny" and through a sort of rite of linguistic inversion thus tend paradoxically to infantilize those to whom they are presenting themselves as grandchildren. The slide from the familiar address "Gramps! Granny!" to the undifferentiated generic term ("the gramps and grannies") follows the same path. Kindness and affection can have degrading effects on their objects by inviting and encouraging them to slip into an exclusive, excluding category, a kind of semantic retirement home where they may feel passive, pampered, and puttering but, in any case, alienated with regard to others.

A short time ago, the press reported on training programs established for caregivers in certain retirement homes to help them "accept the need for intimacy among increasingly sexually liberated residents." It was enlightening to read an article in *Le Monde* on this subject.[1] It revealed the attitude of the nursing staff and, indirectly, the forms of organization that prevail in these homes. One nursing aide stated that the training was very valuable to her: "It's not easy to see one old person kissing another one. Before, that shocked us a bit, now I let it go." It is that officiousness that seems shocking. But things get worse. What, in fact, was the intended outcome of the conferences, exchanges, discussion groups, and other training sessions? The director of one establishment proposed that "eventually" couples and spouses of residents could be accommodated "in adjoining rooms or rooms equipped with double beds." In other words, the present rule is one of authoritarian separation of couples the moment they set foot in this reserve for "dependent" old people. It is not a question of the right to love and sex, as the article seems to conclude, but, more fundamentally, one of individual freedom. Without being ironic about such measures, which are trying to head "in the right direction," as the expression goes, we can take stock of the situation they are attempting to redirect. Must dependent old people be always and only that? Are they less sentient than my cats? There is every reason to fear that the best intentions in the world are pushing them to give up all desire for independence as quickly as possible and give in to servitude.

Conversely, we have long had evidence of overestimating the virtues of old age. Stereotypes on the wisdom born of experience have long been part of the rhetoric of aging. The extension of the average life span dealt them a fatal blow; at least in the West, great age has become commonplace and has lost its exceptional quality. It alone no longer ensures prestige. In our image-driven society, to have any media value, it is necessary to beat the records for longevity (by definition, a fleeting glory) or achieve feats (athletic, dramatic, literary, or political . . .) despite one's age—in short, the exceptional few confirming the gramps-granny rule. In our times, the prestige of old age comes only with one's apparent youthfulness. It immediately falls under the sign of denial.

Without denying anything, and especially not the obvious, can't we question a category of thinking about age that, under the guise of objectivity and quantification, can result in dramatic exclusions from full social life, that is, individual, conscious, social life? Can we decide by decree the degree of lucidity and intelligence of a human being?

The question of age is experienced by all of us in all its aspects and at every age. It is the essential human experience, the meeting place of self and others shared by all cultures, but it is a complex, contradictory place, in which each of us could, if we had the patience and courage, take stock of the half-lies and half-truths that burden our lives. At some time or another, from one point of view or another, each of us is led to question ourselves about our age and thus to become the ethnologists of our own lives.

AS AGE
APPROACHES

O enemy old age! . . .
—CORNEILLE, *LE CID*, ACT 1, SCENE 4

As age approaches, it is much better to welcome it, because it is a sensitive animal and could be tempted to make whomever pretends not to acknowledge it pay dearly for that silence. It does not lack means for demonstrating its presence; better to stroke it the right way and look it in the eye. In short, as age approaches, it is best to proclaim that it is welcome, to swallow your pride and humbly, enthusiastically list the gifts that, like Santa Claus, it will generously pull out of its sack. Essentially and in no order, they are: wisdom born of experience, the tranquility that replaces the torments of the libido, the joys of study, and delight in small everyday pleasures. In short, to treat age as the Ancients treated their goddesses of vengeance, the Erinyes, by calling them the "Eumenides," the "Kindly Ones": eliminating the fear of age by evoking its alleged benefits.

That is the message that Cicero, then sixty-three years old, tried to convey to his friend Atticus, sixty-six years old, by writing *On Old Age*, his *De Senectute*, even as he added to it no small promise: that of immortality. All great men, he claimed, believed in immortality. Not to be too conspicuous about including himself in that category, Cicero chose the literary form of the dialogue and attributed the essence of his remarks to Cato the Older, eighty-four years old. Thus his *De Senectute* is a double fiction; he presents a character who has been dead for a century, and, although he took pleasure in the refuge of writing, his life in that period hardly corresponded to the serene ideal that he sketches out. It included two divorces in two years, the death of his daughter Tullia between them, and political intrigue that would eventually lead to his ruin a few months later. Following the Ides of March, he sided with Octavian and, in the aftermath of the Triumvirate, was assassinated by Antony's soldiers, at the age of sixty-four.

That said, Cicero's text includes two interesting bits of information that can usefully inform any discussion on age and the aged. Old age, it conveys first to Cato, has no monopoly on feebleness and bad health; those things can affect young men. As for old men, they must take care of their physical and intellectual health; those who revert to childhood in their old age were already naturally weak-minded. Of course old age brings to a halt certain activities, but it exerts no harmful effect on the minds of those who carefully maintain their vitality. In sum: tell me how you age, and I will tell you what you were.

> Sophocles composed tragedies to extreme old age, and when, because of his absorption in literary work, he was thought to be neglecting his business affairs, his sons hauled him into court in order to secure a verdict removing him from the control of his property on the ground of imbecility, under a law similar to ours, whereby it is customary to restrain heads of families from wasting their estates. Thereupon, it is said, the old man read to the jury his play, *Oedipus at Colonus*, which he had just written and was revising, and inquired: "Does this poem seem to you to be the work of an imbecile?" When he was finished he was acquitted by the verdict of the jury.[1]

The second piece of information expands upon the aristocratic thinking of the first. If old people are less suited than the young to working life, they are naturally more capable of running things. As Cicero imagines him, Cato comes close to arguing for a gerontocracy. At the same time, the contradiction that subverts all discussion on age is heavily stressed: the frailty accrued with old age on the one hand, the great experience old age might possess on the other. This contradiction, as we know, is only apparent and in fact conceals a class conflict that Cicero never considered hiding, even though he used neither the word nor the concept, and that Simone de

Beauvoir would have every opportunity to highlight in her 1970 book *Old Age*.

All the givens and assumptions behind the remarks made by Cicero two thousand years ago are not really strange to us today, nor are their apparent contradictions. From time to time, the news offers us examples of family disputes over the management of large fortunes, even if those whose autonomy is threatened have a hard time following Sophocles' example and presenting literary works in their own defense. More generally, we must still admit that, despite the growing average life span, the age at which one becomes old depends upon one's social origin and type of occupation. The relationship to age is an expression of social inequality. From this perspective, it must be recognized that the only solution to the problem of dependence would be the eventual education of everyone—a utopia that would not resolve all life's happenstances but would confer on the majority a real chance to exercise their free will.

Life expectancy is also a marker of inequalities between continents and an indicator of development. As ethnologist and traveler, I continually encountered old people who, I could sometimes verify, were younger than me even though I was still not very old. In Sub-Saharan Africa, to attain a relatively advanced age is a sign of power. The first time that someone called me "Old Man!" in the Ivory Coast, I was not yet forty, and I was flattered by this sign of respect. Exactly the opposite of the angry dismay that overtook me much later, the day an unfortunate young man thought it was a good idea to make a show of offering me his seat in the Métro.

Intellectuals are more capable than others of responding to Cicero's wish to see old people maintain their minds as much as their bodies. In this regard, they benefit from a kind of guaranteed income that they are charged with making last. This "pension" is not without ambiguities, moreover, because it falls more to them than to others to provide the proof that they are worthy of it. As age approaches, they may well fear that their writing or their slightest remarks will be scrutinized with particularly critical attention to detect the first signs of senescence. Thus perhaps resulting, for some, in attempts to show off and to embellish content and form, to become more radical in their old age, which would only be to reverse dramatically the course that usually makes the rebels of the past into the conservatives of the future. And we may be tempted to read this astonishing cry on the lips of a few merry old gents: "Younger than me? You die!"

Liking easy contrasts, television encourages the slightly theatrical appearance of these temporal hybrids, these video-acoustic bats ("I'm wise, look at my white hair; I'm young, listen to what I say"). But theirs is no easy task. It is hard for them to condemn the gerontocratic ideal advocated by Cicero and Cato because that denouncement itself, coming from them, could easily pass, in the guise of preserved or rediscovered youth, as a claim to authority, as a coy claim to wisdom, experience, and power, at the very least the power of influence. But before passing

judgment on those who play up their age, let us acknowledge a few extenuating circumstances.

If they "act their age," it is because, with more or less
malice, ingenuousness, or tact, it is too often thrown in
their faces. A little like those foreigners who are asked
where they come from by anyone who detects a slight
accent in their speech and thus feels authorized, the old
person arouses the curiosity of the bus rider, the taxi
driver, the television host. Age is to aging intellectuals what beauty is to women. It would never occur to a
television host to praise the attractive figure of a male
actor (that type of compliment is reserved for women);
likewise, it would never occur to him to go ecstatic over
the age of a forty-year-old (that type of compliment is
reserved for the old). The euphemisms of the official language (third age, fourth age) only add to the ambient dis-
comfort, as though certain words prompt fear. A converse
popularizing promotes certain adjectives like "young" to
the status of nouns. "The young are nervous about their
future." When I was young, this grammatical shift was
reserved for "old," and one spoke crudely of the "retirement of the old," which meant the minimal pension of
those without resources. "The old" corresponded to a social class, a bit like "the young" does today.

The best way to avoid being assigned to a general category is, as we know, to "reverse the stigma," but there
is also the attempt at seduction through denial that can
paradoxically accompany it. With regard to old age, we
see these two mechanisms at work, certainly among a
few relatively prominent media personalities but also in

conversations at bars or over family meals, in the form of an opposition between what is and what seems. "I am not who you think I am . . ." is the key phrase in all attempts at seduction: "Thus, seek in me that other whom you don't know." In this instance is added the recognition that age is understood not to encompass the whole person, thus the "I'm old, but . . ." ("I'm old, but I'm not finished," "I'm old, but I have more than one string to my bow . . ."). And even more, there is the claim of age understood as a trump card, thus the "I'm old, but that's precisely . . ." ("I'm old, but that's precisely what makes me free . . . ," "I'm old, but that's precisely what lets me understand youth . . ."). This denial in the form of allusion is eminently true in part, because no one is reduced to the simple appearance of one's age, as long as a bit of consciousness remains. But likening memory to a form of experience, which is implicit in all the lessons dispensed by the aged in the name of their age, is more questionable and falls under fiction, under the reinvention of self to which we are all tempted to succumb at one time or another.

In this respect, professional actors are more directly condemned to honesty than writers or intellectuals because the roles they agree to perform, which they do not write, are largely dependent upon their physical appearance and their age. As paradoxical as this assertion may at first seem, the actors themselves are not free to hide behind the cloak of language. Even if their makeup gives them some room to maneuver, we appreciate the ability of the greatest actors and actresses to embody characters who are always their age over the course of their lives. It is by aging that they renew themselves. It is true that life's fortunes sometimes produce brilliant fireworks in the area of literary creation as in the dramatic arts: Raymond Radiguet, James Dean. . . . But these effects stem from the indifferent suddenness of death that cuts down lives in their prime and creates legends in which the author is confused with his work or the actor with his role through the magic of a displacement that is as much metonymic as metaphoric. On the other hand, there is nothing sadder than the descending trajectory of those stars who, in their own time and through the luck and brilliance of youth, become myths and then never stop aging in trying to survive them.

The actor who continues to act usually takes roles that correspond to his age; he does not introduce conflict between his life and his craft. As his roles are renewed, it is always a new experience for him; he is revived without repeating himself. The writer and the intellectual are more exposed, to the extent that, to avoid repeating themselves, they may be tempted by false youth and force their words as others dye their hair in colors claimed to be natural. Thus we can conclude that talent, in both cases, is greatest when it coincides with a taste for truth—which, in short, is comforting.

HOW OLD
ARE YOU?

"I am of age and vaccinated."

"**Q**uel âge avez-vous?" This question is even more awkward in a language like English, which uses the auxiliary verb "to be": not "What age *have* you?" but "How old *are* you?" And the response is even worse: "I am. . . ." Am I really these forty, fifty, sixty or more years by which I am thus condemned to define myself? In one sense, yes, and it is others, society, and its rules that decide that sense. Age requirements are established in every domain: coming of age, retirement, candidacy for the Académie Française—as if, past a certain age, one can no longer aspire to immortality—but also, determined by sperm banks, the age limit for a woman and her partner to aspire to medically assisted procreation. A cardinal can no longer participate in the conclave to elect a pope once he has turned eighty. In short, what is most deeply personal to me, my degree of advancement in time, which draws me closer to death, *my* death, is registered, managed, and subjected to rules, dispensations, and exceptions: if I am my age, and am only my age, I am essentially a social and cultural being, strictly defined by collectively recognized rules. But does this accumulation of rules really concern me? Did I truly stop being a "minor" at the age of twenty-one? Does this transformation really take place three years earlier nowadays? Did I become someone else once I retired? Do I no longer have anything to say beginning from sixty-five, seventy, or eighty years old? One problem with freedom, and even more so with life expectancy increasing: the number taken out of circulation threatens to grow.

A danger of these rules: when will old people be forbidden from voting?

And from the reverse perspective, aren't we seeing childhood's portion shrinking? Is a criminal under sixteen years old truly a minor or evidence of the particularly tragic kind of erosion that more generally affects the shores of adolescence? It remains true nonetheless that over the course of a life one crosses thresholds, even if they are recognized only in retrospect, even if they vary according to the individual and also the area of occupation. One can simultaneously be an old tennis player and a young executive or cabinet member.

I once heard an old woman tell me in her own language and with a charming smile that she had retained "her young girl's soul." I think I understand what she meant. That behind the wrinkles, the body's wear and tear, there was the same outlook, the same sensibility, a form of permanence. Maybe it is this discrepancy between the aging of the body and the longevity of subjective psychology that prompted the establishment of a distinction between body and soul, which seems obvious and natural to many and makes them believe, more or less vaguely, in the immortality of a spiritual principle.

"How old are you?" For a while now, I have found that question awkward. First of all, for those asking it, because it seems to me evidence of a kind of indelicacy that I did not suspect. And then because I have to think before answering. What to say? I know my age, I can state it, but I do not believe it. Two clarifications nonetheless. When old compatriots ask it, this question does not prompt that mute irritation in me; we are more or less the same age, and they already know the answer. But we sometimes take pleasure in reviewing the details, finding out who is the elder by a few weeks, even a few days, pretending as if we were in competition and trying to establish the pecking order. We joke, and in a certain way this mockery corresponds to our state of mind: we are old, but we do not always realize it, as though our parallel displacement together in the same time and direction has made us unconscious of movement. Second clarification: this trouble I have stating my age is relatively recent, at least in this form. After I turned thirty-five, the approach of forty sometimes made me nervous. Once out of that area of turbulence, that air pocket, I regained altitude and age without particular emotion. It was when

I became older than my father, who died when he was sixty-four, that I began to feel "beyond age." And without any particular distress and not the least desire for denial, I no longer identified with my age, whether, according to the subtle distinction of the INSEE (National Institute of Statistics and Economic Studies), it was the age "achieved in the year" or the age "in years that had passed."

Age is the length of time that has passed since birth. It can be calculated according to two definitions:
—the age by generation or age achieved in the year,
—the age in years that have passed.
The age generally used is the age achieved in the year. It corresponds to the difference between the year in question and the year of birth for the individual.
The age in years that have passed is the age at the last birthday. Thus, on the date in question, in the same generation, the age in years that have passed is not the same for all individuals.
For example, an individual born on October 10, 1925 dies on April 18, 1999. He is 74 years old in the age achieved in the year: 1999 minus 1925 equals 74. But he is 73 years old in years that have passed: April 18, 1999 minus October 10, 1925 equals 73 years 6 months and 8 days.[1]

These distinctions on the INSEE website may seem obvious, but they correspond to various strategic possibilities for those who are asked their age. My grandfather had a way of stating his age that was a kind of synthesis of INSEE's two methods of calculation. He started with his birthday in the following year and did an ordinal breakdown. "I am on the brink of entering my eighty-first year," he declared the day of his seventy-ninth birthday. He had two ambitions: to survive his sisters-in-law and to become the village elder. He achieved them both, but his propensity to make himself older always struck me as responding to a kind of humorous vertigo in the face of the acceleration of the final years.

For my part, I feel more "beyond age." *Hors d'âge*: the expression used for old armagnacs conveys that it is not a matter of denying the weight of time, very much to the contrary. An armagnac *hors d'âge* results from bringing together many very old armagnacs. An individual *hors d'âge* brings together many pasts not equally present in his memory, reconstructed pasts, and often the oldest ones are not the least tenacious and can give him the impression that his life has passed in a flash, whereas others, more recent but already fading, might easily convince him of having lived for an eternity, and still others drift in an indistinct haze at the edge of his memory, so that he can neither situate nor date them precisely: "Souvenirs? More than if I had lived a thousand years!" writes Baudelaire in *Les fleurs du mal*.[2]

The reference to armagnac is deceptive, of course. It would seem to suggest that the mixing of times necessarily results in a form of excellence, thus reintroducing the ambiguities around the notion of experience. Whereas here, the expression "beyond age" is meant simply to apply to the multiplicity of times present in each of us at every instant and even more so when we try to "take stock," to "pause for a moment." In the detailed account of the years gone by, we are so far from finding a guiding principle, or even a general orientation, the irregular thread that would allow us to follow the course of the past and to appreciate its relative coherence retrospectively. Instead we find ourselves confronted with a fluid, composite mass where, among certain factual elements in our memories, which are also the memories of our hopes, expectations, and disappointments, there are a few holes that give a strange inconsistency to the days past, an awareness of external constraints of all kinds that weighed on our lives to the point of making us sometimes doubt that they were really ours. And finally there is the premonition that our future will not follow in an orderly way from our present any more than our present has from our past, which precedes but escapes it. In short, exactly the opposite of a curriculum vitae or a career plan, and sometimes the shadow of a doubt about our singular, individual identity.

AUTOBIOGRAPHY AND ETHNOLOGY OF SELF

"It's no more than your age!"

Literary autobiography seems less driven by a narcissistic temptation to talk about oneself than a desire to fix oneself in time with a few incontestable pieces of evidence, a bit like those tourists who seem more anxious to photograph the landscape or sights pointed out to them than actually to look at them. Given the fleeting nature of the moment and the least event, the most important thing is to anticipate being able to see it again in order to believe it, to anticipate the absence that already looms, the shadow cast by an elusive present. This is the opposite of what is sometimes called the work of grieving, which tends to allay the forgetting. It is not a question of admitting that the other is no longer there but of assuring oneself of having been there, in person.

There are many kinds of autobiographies. Some are more or less like log books, in which what is recounted is contemporaneous with the writing. Others are closer to memoirs, in which references to the present are not necessarily absent, but it is past events that are explicitly related. The question of age is approached from different perspectives.

In his journal, the autobiographer depicts himself in very nearly the present moment, like those travelers who pose before the pyramids or Notre Dame. They carefully note the place and date. They each want to be sure of having existed on such-and-such a day in such-and-such a year. But the autobiographer has the advantage over the photographed tourists of a double existence: as the author of the text and as the subject depicted. Thus he may be exposed to a double surprise later, if he can no longer find himself in the first or recognize himself in the second. He might just as well do as Michel Leiris does in *Manhood*, that is, to push the detail of that snapshot to the extreme and without mercy, making it more faithful and more severe than any simple photo ID.

I have just reached the age of thirty-four, life's mid-point. Physically, I am of average height, on the short side. I have my auburn hair cut short to keep it from curling, and also to prevent the spread of an incipient baldness. . . . I like to dress with the greatest possible elegance; yet due to the defects I have just described in my physique and to my financial means, which, without my being able to

call them poor, are rather limited, I usually consider myself profoundly inelegant; I loathe unexpectedly catching
sight of myself in a mirror, for unless I have prepared
myself for the confrontation, I seem humiliatingly ugly to
myself each time.[1]

Despite the title he gave his "autobiography," *L'âge
d'homme*, it is not age that interests Leiris, but time.
He is part of the branch of literature on time, not the
branch on age. Walter Benjamin clearly understood that
L'âge d'homme was above all an investigation of self, not
an expression of nostalgia or a meditation on maturity.
Leiris's voice seems to strain a bit when he says he is at
"life's mid-point." Interested in the "metaphysics" of his
childhood and the myths of his youth, he is searching
primarily for the key to an essential hesitation that, he
thinks, defines him once and for all. When he plunges
into life's events, dreams, or readings, his only aim is to
find the best way of defining and expressing those endless swings between "good" and "bad," tranquility and
motion. He is Merlin the wizard lost in the forest of Bro-
celiande and held prisoner by Viviane under the effects
of the magic that he himself taught her:

Often, as I reflected on this story, it seemed to me a kind
of image of my own life—the life of a man who gorged
himself on pessimism, believing he would find in it a
means to a dazzling and meteoric existence, loving his
own despair until the day he realized—too late—that

he could no longer emerge from it, and that he had thus
fallen into the trap of his own enchantments.

More specifically, according to Walter Benjamin, this
trap may be psychoanalysis, with its sterilizing effects
on literary output. That is the lesson he draws from Leiris's confidences in this regard: "It is indeed unlikely that
a man who was led to do such scrupulous psychic inven-
tories could retain hope of future works."[2] Except that,
perhaps, Leiris's experience of psychoanalysis seems
very much to have had precisely the status of an experience in an enterprise the whole of which he grasped only
gradually and retrospectively, as is often the case. His inquiry focuses on himself, to be sure, but beyond that, on
the question of being, which his experience as an ethnologist helps reformulate, especially through his studies
on the phenomenon of possession. Rereading him today
can give us the impression that his eminently literary
works belong less to the domain of psychology and psychoanalysis than to ethnology, an ethnology of the self.
To prove to himself that he exists, Leiris finds a kind of
confirmation and justification in the ethnology of others.

The repetitions, recurrences, and indecisions evoked
in *Manhood*, which Leiris catalogues by arranging them
under two opposing and complementary figures: Lucre-
tia, the virtuous, violated Roman woman whose suicide
led to the fall of the monarchy, and Judith, the Jewish
heroine who prompted the Assyrians' defeat by seduc-
ing and assassinating Holofernes, have a very literary
mode of existence. They also constitute so many indirect

responses to the nagging question that reappears end-lessly in various guises under the author's pen: Who am I? An echo anticipated by another inquiry growing out of surrealism, which will let us appreciate the sentry's injunction in Julien Gracq's *The Opposing Shore*: "Who lives?" Echo as well of the interrogation found formulat-ed a thousand ways in the rituals of possession: no lon-ger simply, Who am I? but beyond and before, What am I? This question stops time; it is for good reason that the possessed must forget the episodes of possession when coming back to themselves.

The feeling of waiting is expressed as it is experienced: it accentuates the contours of the present so strongly that it can give the impression of suspending time. At first glance, there is nothing of this *suspense* for Leiris, because he explores scenes from childhood and youth he has undoubtedly relived a thousand times. Yet these two opposing impulses are both searching for the form of an enigma in the material of time. Who am I, who was I? Who goes there, who lives? Who is there? Who will come? What am I—an illusion, a memory, an absence, a desire? The present of *suspense* is so strong that, for the time being, it eliminates the possibility of any sequel or es-cape. For its part, the inquiry on self proceeds by a series of freeze-frames that erase any reference to duration, to passage or age: nothing less biographic, in the end, than autobiography thus conceived.

Writing that takes on time as its subject tries to re-store its specific sensual delights: not the past as such, but the refinements of memory or forgetting; not childhood, but what it already foretells of the uncertainties of adulthood; not history, but the rare moments when it can seem to brush up against or engulf the writer's history; not the war, but, as in Gracq's *A Balcony in the Forest*, the new experiences of waiting that it occasioned.

When writing is more concerned with age (as with an author like Stefan Zweig in *The World of Yesterday: Memories of a European*, for example), the influence of history is exerted more directly on the account of the life; chronology, the stages of existence, more clearly mark the personal journey. Literature on age is more attuned to the tragedies of existence and more nostalgic for paradises lost. When, in 1940, Zweig evokes the Paris he discovered in 1904, his pages are moving for many reasons. First of all because in 1940 "the swastika hung from the Eiffel Tower." Zweig, exiled in Brazil, would commit suicide a few months later. His memoirs are a recapitulation of events that counted for him, a bit like some people on their deathbeds are said to see their lives pass before them, a fast-forward of the major episodes in their existence. The Paris that he remembers, the Paris of his youth, the Paris of 1904 was a completely ideal world—the distinctions of class were less rigid, those of race nonexistent, women were free, everyone was happy: "Chinese and Scandinavians, Spaniards and Greeks, Brazilians and Canadians, all felt themselves at home on the banks of the Seine." The enchanting depiction of this dream of Paris moves us for two contradictory reasons: because it represents a lost dream and because, as idealized as it obviously is, it certainly contains an element of truth that, now more than ever, awakens regrets. Human beings age, and cities do as well. The Paris of 1904 that Zweig sees again is undoubtedly an illusion, but a Paris existed that was capable of giving birth to that illusion, and I am not sure that today's Paris still possesses that poetic power.

For a moment I experience a similar illusion when I think back to Paris following the Liberation. Everyone seemed to me happy and full of joy. I was ten years old in 1945. In the streets there was whistling (who still whistles in the streets these days?). In my head, I still have a thousand refrains from the songs of that time. It was the era of radio talent shows and from various spots in Paris, Saint-Granier hosted a broadcast called *On Chante dans mon Quartier*—"They Sing in My Neighborhood" (*ploum ploum tralala, voilà c'qu'on chante chez moi*—"ho hum tralala, that's what they sing where I live"). To my eyes, there was general euphoria; children ran after American soldiers of all colors to ask them, in English, for chewing gum and chocolate, which the liberators distributed by the handful, smiling. This depiction of a dream Paris where I am sure of having lived is the best illustration that can be offered of the past as definitively past; that juncture of a moment in my life and a moment in history will never happen again. Thus what strikes me today is less the partly illusory, subjective nature of the impression of general euphoria that I felt in that period than the certainty that it is gone forever.

When Zweig dreams of Paris, that luminous place gives depths to his depiction of the years gone by and emphasizes their impossible, irreparable weight. He is caught up by the obvious fact of age, by the sinister present, and by the seemingly irreversible nature of his experience of exile. The year 1904 will not come again. The subject of his memoirs is not first and foremost a search for the self, but the passage of time, which, in this tragic century, and for some more than others, merges with history—history punctuated with pauses, accelerations, and dramatic turns of events.

As he summarizes it in his last book, Zweig's life is nevertheless the stuff of fiction, in the sense that there is always something passive in fiction: a form of waiting that, depending on the circumstances, can resemble fascination, terror, curiosity, or hope. Passivity with regard to age that inevitably arrives: "So the years passed with work and travel, with study, reading, collecting, and enjoying life. One morning in November 1931, I woke to find myself fifty years old."[3] Passivity with regard to success, a kind of surprise about the vast amount of work he had authored and the audience that read it. Impatience as well about knowing what would follow, presented in this case both as personal (in terms of the work yet to be produced) and as triggered by an external event, by history: "So on my fiftieth birthday, deep within myself I had but one wicked wish—for something would tear me away from all these guarantees and comforts, that would necessitate my not merely continuing, but my starting anew." When he wrote those lines in 1941, Zweig had already decided to kill himself, and he wondered where, a few years earlier, that wish for a different, more difficult life had come from, which had been granted but which, he admitted, had never been a matter of a conscious desire: "It was no more than a passing thought that blew my way, perhaps not even my own thought but rather one that came from depths I knew nothing of."

We may be tempted to assume that the reference to this "passing thought" has a retrospective dimension, that it notes a historical inevitability, and that the premonition it reports is closer to a realization after the fact of the irremediable nature of the interdependence tragically binding a personal history to history itself.

Of course, by definition, memoirs are never contemporaneous with the events they report, and their retrospective vision conditions the way in which they evoke time, age, and the future. But some writers choose to write memoirs, others to keep journals, while others think of themselves expressly as autobiographers, and still others maintain their distance from any conscious, explicit reference to their biography.

Simone de Beauvoir combines two methods of recording time, the journal and the memoir, for *The Prime of Life*—which relates episodes during and immediately after the war—by using notebooks in which, following Sartre's example, she wrote down events and impressions. Beginning in September 1939 (war was declared, Sartre mobilized), she kept a journal for a few months, some pages of which she incorporated into her account ("And then one morning the thing happened. Then, in solitude and anguish, I began to keep a journal . . ."). From which derives the double tempo of the book overall: in the background of the picture, the war, whose horrors and consequences she, like her readers, knew in 1960, the year the book was published. But first of all, in the foreground, history experienced on the individual, everyday level, which retains something innocent and anecdotal. For the most part, Beauvoir is on the side of time, not of age. Double *suspense*: stemming from the war, of course, but from a war experienced, in the midst of a kind of long vacation, as a play in which actors cross, in which some disappear suddenly (Lautman, Cavaillès, Nizan, Desnos . . .), dragged into a history other than her own, but also, and even more so, to become her own, undoubtedly because, as for Leiris, whom she encountered also in those years, and for Sartre, obviously, the interior adventure is, despite everything, the most compelling one (what am I going to write? what am I going to become?), without the temptation of taking risks ever emerging, at least in any pronounced way and despite the context, or the idea of a possible death.

The two inflections of time and age are present in all authors, in variable proportions. Even those who keep or have kept a journal sometimes feel the need to distance themselves from this way of reporting the succession of days, to take stock and to question, shifting, for example, from the delight they feel in "embracing their time" to a more or less uneasy reflection on the fact that it is over and they have aged. We may think here especially of Claude Mauriac returning to his journal of many decades, *Le temps immobile*. Or once again of Simone de Beauvoir, who gives her age (fifty years old) in the prologue of *The Prime of Life* precisely to justify both having written the account of her first twenty years in *Memoirs of a Dutiful Daughter* and now providing a sequel to it with this new book, which she had not initially foreseen. In the first case, it was a matter, she says, of giving life back to an adolescent who would otherwise disappear forever:

> Nor did I ever forget the distress signals which my adolescent self sent out to the older woman who was afterward to absorb me, body and soul. Nothing, I feared, would survive of that girl, not so much as a pinch of ashes. I begged her successor to recall my youthful ghost, one day, from the limbo to which it had been consigned. Perhaps the only reason for writing my books was to make the fulfillment of this long-standing prayer possible.[4]

In the second case, she adds, it was a matter of giving a meaning to this story in the form of genesis: "There was no point in having described how my vocation as a writer was acquired unless I then went on to show its realization."

As with Leiris, observing time is first of all a tool of self-inquiry; the mention of age is only a reference point in the observation of the self. A deliberate, voluntary, conscious note: "I feel that I am becoming somehow well-defined; I am going to be thirty-two years old, I feel as if I am a woman fully made, I would love to know which," Simone de Beauvoir writes in her journal on November 4, 1939.

Memoir or journal, in any case, an account of another's life holds the attention of numerous readers. No doubt precisely because of this double tempo—or, if you prefer, this "double talk," without denying the role of duplicity implicit in that expression—because it is also their life, and because they rediscover it in the writing of another, with a feeling of recognition, in both senses of the word. They recognize themselves there—or, at the very least, they recognize something of their own ambivalence in the apprehension of time—and they are grateful to the author. Double talk? In fact, there is in each of us an inner voice that sometimes expresses itself in murmurs, muttering, onomatopoeias, facial contractions, or, more rarely (when "we are talking to ourselves"), in the form of a few articulated words. It comments on our most everyday reality, heckles us, sometimes judges us in harsh terms (What an idiot I am!); in short, it is the verbalized expression of our "beyond age" consciousness, of that ordinary reflexiveness that has always accompanied the course of our existence and that puts us at a distance from ourselves, that preserves in each of us that part of free-floating attention that eludes fate, accident, and age. If I say to myself, a little disillusioned, "Oh well, my old man, you're not getting any younger . . . ," I recognize myself without identifying with myself, I put myself to one side, as if I were the author of this character who escapes me a little even as I never lose sight of him. The presence of this divided consciousness may explain why we are not surprised by the usual device that the novel depends upon (an omniscient author who transcends the subjectivity of his characters) and why, in fact, we are tempted to perceive in many novels a more or less rough metaphor for our own lives.

Rereading Simone de Beauvoir, evoking Sartre and Leiris, I spontaneously call up a part of Paris where I lived for a long time and a bit of history that marked me for life, even though I was a child when these authors reached maturity. Later, I happened to interview them, but the image that their writings created in me, as vague as it may be, remains the most persistent one. It almost ranks as a memory, which speaks volumes about what a memory is. That composite, where I also rediscover many places I frequented in different time periods, surprisingly precise details about life in the 1940s, and the invigorating energy that reading *The Prime of Life* instilled in me at the age of twenty-five, speaks volumes about me, in one sense, but it speaks to me alone. Again, we must agree on the word "speak." If I am incapable of transcribing that speech, that is because it is not a matter of syntactically articulated language. Perhaps instead it is a matter of an intuition on the poetic order, which establishes unexpected contact between remote elements that do not seem destined to come together. But that poem will never be written or read. I alone will hear it, incapable as I am of even humming it to myself. We are all bearers of such poems, which resist age because they are made only of time.

Thus it is a question of time as material, time that we shape as we please, that we compose and recompose, time that we play with for the pleasure of it. When old friends meet again and exchange memories, they know very well that they will never recapture the flavor of the old days, and moreover, that is a good thing: they were often quite dull. But they rediscover something of the pleasure of exchange, something that locates them at a distance from aging and the passing time:

"I believe that was the best time we ever had," said Frédéric.

"Well, perhaps, yes, I too believe that was the best time we ever had," said Deslauriers.[5]

Let us remember that they are recalling their pathetic youthful expedition to the Turkish brothel in Nogent. The end of *Sentimental Education* literally conveys the disenchantment of two friends, one returning after political illusion, the other after romantic illusion, but both finding themselves, by some sort of default, doubly disillusioned. Isn't a sentimental education first of all a formative, perhaps selfish, experience in forgetting, which allows you to find yourself again—an experience of time not to be confused with one of age? Moreover there is a feeling of complicity in the disenchantment that makes it similar to "reunions," that is to say, the rebirth of a relationship. This is neither glorious or truly hopeless. The results constitute a failure but also the possible beginning of another story.

Leiris and Beauvoir are not so far removed. Nor Rousseau and his *Reveries of the Solitary Walker*. The writing of autobiography or memoir is comparable to the effect of time on ruins: it works by means of subtraction and selection. Thus it suggests that behind all original creation there is a portion of forgetting or, at the very least, a relationship with time that removes all relevance from the distinction between memory and forgetting, something like a rediscovery or, as in the case of the ritual when it is successful, a renewal. No doubt writing plays this part with regard to the life that passes and passes away, that is, with regard to age. Writing plays the role of ritual when ritual is effective and manages to give those participating or attending the feeling that it reopens time.

Could I but end my days in this charming isle, without evermore stirring from it, or seeing a single inhabitant of the continent, who could remind me of all those calamities which have for so many years united to overwhelm me! . . . Delivered from every worldly passion the tumult of social life engenders, my soul would frequently rise above this atmosphere, and, before-hand, converse with those celestial beings whose number it hopes soon to increase. Men will take care, I know, not to give back so sweet an asylum from which they already have taken me; but they cannot prevent me from daily conveying myself there on the wings of the imagination, and tasting the same pleasure as when I was really there. All I should do with more delight would be to think with more ease. In imagining I am there, is it not the same thing? It is even more; to the charm of an abstract and monotone meditation, I join delightful images which enliven it. Their objects often escaped my senses during my ecstasy, and now, the more my meditations are profound, the greater expression they give them. I am often more amongst them, and more agreeably too, than when I was there in reality. The misfortune is, that still my imagination weakens, these things strike me more slowly and stay but a short while. Alas! 'tis when we begin to leave this body it most offends the mind.[6]

Rousseau wrote his *Reveries* beginning in 1776 in Paris and in Ermenonville, where he died in 1778. The end of the fifth walk summarizes much mental activity, many flights of the soul, that the author's reflections, at the very moment of his writing, seem to make issue forth from one another: first of all, his longing in remembering the island of Saint-Pierre, and more specifically the moments of escape into reverie that he experienced there; the almost simultaneous recognition that he can always abandon himself to that reverie—even though it is now only through the imagination that he reexperiences the ebb and flow of the lake waters that then gave his existence a feeling of physicality; immediately afterward, the remark that his daydream is more complete in the moment when he is writing than ten years earlier, since it enhances the mixture of presence and escape that constitutes his "ecstasies," the "delightful images" of the place of welcome and its hosts; finally the mention of the aging body, which, on the other hand, limits and weakens the power of the imagination and vividness of memory.

Despite this last remark, made almost lightly, and despite the wounds from which he still suffers, the author of *Reveries* displays a remarkable serenity here; it is the calm after the storm, the evening glow, the feeling perhaps that despite everything, something was accomplished. Two references to age (the memory of persecutions to which he was subjected "for so many years" and the approach of the moment when he will have to "leave this body") thus frame the evocation of a nonlinear time in which the after can be richer and more precise than the before, a time that remains in the face of time that passes, a time that provides pleasure and happiness.

Rousseau wrote. Writing is the tool that allowed him to substitute time for age. As we know, Rousseau left his *Reveries* unfinished, death quickly claimed him, but it is the fate of all great work to be forever unfinished. It offers itself to readers to whom it expressly appeals and for whom its very existence mitigates the importance of age. Over the course of time, their successive readings will question and enrich it. Thus the work will no longer belong to the author; he will be dispossessed of it. We could even say that the author will no longer belong to himself either—which corresponds to the most modest and ambitious of dreams he is able to formulate and to the wisest and wildest illusion he can maintain: to ignore age and let time run its course.

To write is to die a little, but a little less alone.

CLASS

"I belong to the class of '55."

Space helps us not only represent but also master, order, and even stop time, or it gives us the feeling of doing so. How old are you? Scarcely have I understood the question and opened my mouth to answer than I have already aged a few seconds; on the other hand, if I pull out my ID card, I find my date of birth inscribed there; that is solid, fixed. Beginning at fifteen years old, children can no longer be listed on their parents' passports; they must have their own. In short, they are entitled to their own dates of birth. In the time when military service existed, one belonged to a "class" named by the number obtained by adding twenty to one's year of birth and retaining the two last digits of the subsequent result. In the twentieth century, someone belonging to the class of '46 was born in 1926, someone belonging to the class of '09 was born in 1889. On the day the draft board conducted their medical exams, all the young men who were twenty years old at the time, who were then still minors, were assembled in a well-established place by the mayor of the town. And they had to strip naked. In short, a second birth.

Stating one's class requires no arithmetic; unlike one's age, it does not change each year. It is an element of one's permanent identity. And also of solidarity, of belonging to a group. In rural areas, I have often heard men talking about someone else and referring to them as being "my class," like they might say "my cousin."

Unlike graduation years at the major universities, class involved a whole generation, nonexclusive and place based. Military service itself could make young men move around; for some, it was even their only opportunity to leave home. But the draft board and the official assignment to a class as such gathered neighbors together. Class is the simultaneous acknowledgment of an individual and a collective identity (a set of relationships), both of them fixed in time and inscribed in space.

In France, the classes of draftees go back only to the Second Empire, and they have lost their symbolic significance since mandatory military service was abolished, but their inner logic is of the same order as that of the African age classes (which also served a military function moreover). What underlies their definition is a circular and recurrent conception of time. Given how they are calculated and named, every hundred years, classes of the same name ought to reappear. Thus, given the extension of human life, we could soon see a few hundred-year-old men timidly joining the class of twenty-year-olds because that class would have the same name as theirs. That was occasionally the case, with smaller age gaps, in certain age class systems in Africa.

Among the Attie, a matrilineal society of the eastern Ivory Coast, there were three large age classes, each divided into five subclasses. Sons belonged to an age class alternating with the one of their fathers. Two brothers could belong to the same class but not to the same subclass. Formerly, this organization was rendered by dividing the area of the village also into three: low, middle, and high. The fathers (the generation in power) occupied the middle area, the sons the low, and the generation in between the high. Denise Paulme thus describes the traditional progression of life for an Attie man:

> The son, born at his father's house, left the paternal home when he became a man, to follow, from the distance of one generation, an identical course that led him from the low area of the village to the high and then to the middle; he ended his days in a residence neighboring the one where he had grown up but always different, the lineage of the son not being the one of the father.[1]

The cyclical organization of age classes was thus conveyed by a circular course in the village space. During the forming of a new age class, an old man who belonged to the class with the same name could be subject to the same ordeals as the children whose equal he became, notes Denise Paulme again. A symbolic way of coming full circle in a world where representations of heredity express a substantial form of continuity between generations in other respects as well.

Officially belonging to an age class means being attached to a specific place. That is very obvious in the age class system, which functions as an instrument of political management for a given space, even if it means an element of internal spatial mobility accompanies it, as is the case among the Attie. It is equally obvious on the individual level. Stages of existence have often been associated with specific, successive places; notions of career and appointment have a geographic dimension that determines the temporal perspective. Giraudoux celebrates the course of the enlisted man receiving orders, who leaves the provinces with the hope of "ascending the ranks" to reach Paris. Beyond that, some individuals are preoccupied by the question of their "old age," which they sometime imagine spending in a rural setting or in a "nursing home." There are few of us who, approaching old age, do not assign a specific geographical framework to our last years. In the Breton branch of my family, many came to "finish out their days" in their native village and, when the family tomb finally ran out of space and could no longer accommodate them, their kin would find them a tomb as close to that one as possible. This native village was not their birthplace in some cases (the Bretons had traveled around the world as soldiers or civil servants, often the rank and file of the colonial "adventure"), but it constituted a landmark and reference point in the logic of age that determined their lives, as among the Attie.

IMAGES D'ÉPINAL

"He passed the milestone of fifty."

"The ages of life" form a pictorial motif that does not correspond to any concrete experience. A memory from our youth does sometimes come back to us, an image that is insistent but fuzzy on the details. However, the succession of scenes evoked by some painters to illustrate the theme of the ages of life, those *Images d'Épinal* that used to decorate French kitchen walls, never file past in our memory. Those representations of the human body rising by degrees toward the prime of life before descending again bent over toward extreme old age elaborate a kind of illustrated cartography upon which each of us can locate ourselves, if we like, in relationship to the ten-year sections that are carved into time there. But this sequence never presents itself as such to the mind of the one who is remembering.

These representations have historical significance; they are marked by their era, and in some of them we can notice, for example, the full blossoming promised to the man of fifty, at the height of his social ascent, whereas the woman, the wife, at the same age, is already assigned to her role of cheerful, aging grandmother. The "ages of life" are undeniably dated.

These images also assume the endurance of a family model that serves to support them. A simplified, basic model that refers simply to the direct line of a single couple: here, lineage is only the normal marker of passing time.

Because I sometimes saw them in my childhood or, later, in a country house here and there, I regard them today with the feeling that outdated objects sometimes inspire in those who paid them only fleeting attention at the time when they were not outdated.

Examining them more closely, however, these innocent scenes seem to act as a screen—in both senses of the word—to a reality that they express and veil at the same time. The stereotype of the bourgeois couple to which the motif of the ages of life corresponds becomes a well-oiled machine: each generation pushes the next one toward the exit. No doubt this is one of the reasons for the latent tension that prevails in the relations between successive generations in many societies (ethnologists have often reported this), and especially when the idea of death is not associated with the idea of renewal, when the wheel turns for everyone but turns only once for each of us. The paradox is that the aggressive tension corresponding to the feeling of being pushed toward death by those immediately following spares those whose birth nevertheless marks the advance of age: grandchildren. It is as if the grandparents are reconciled to aging by the idea that their own children are going to be subjected in turn to the tensions inherent in the relations between parent and child, which also inspires in them gratitude with regard to their grandchildren.

My grandfather called the whole passel of his grandchildren "the little avengers." He was kidding, of course, but neither his sons nor his daughters-in-law fully appreciated his irony.

The question is not whether parents love their children more or less than grandparents love their grandchildren. As a general rule, of course, they all love one another, but love is a complex feeling that does not exclude resentment or jealousy or possessiveness; nor does it exclude the taste for power or the awareness of economic interests. Tensions express themselves more strongly between two successive generations directly engaged with each other than between alternate generations related less directly and more disinterestedly. Moreover, we know the Oedipal dimension is always present, which creates ambivalent love/rivalry relations particularly between mother and daughter on one side and father and son on the other.

49 | IMAGES D'ÉPINAL

As a child, Leiris saw an illustration representing the ages of life. But, if his memories are accurate, it was a matter of a specific version, on the back cover of a picture album published in Épinal. Each age was associated with a color—yellow, gray, red, green, blue . . .—and the whole thing was entitled *The Colors of Life.* He remembers in particular the color "*meli-melo*" mixing many shades and evoking the chaos of early childhood when everything is still indistinct, like in mythic times, as well as the color "*marrons cuit*," "chestnut brown," the caption for an image of two drunk tramps. The lesson that he draws from this vague memory is ambiguous. He notes, not without humor, that he has already passed "through a certain number of these colors, including, long before forty, that of chestnut brown." We can see that from all the colors in life, this is the lesson Leiris seems to draw from his uncertain memory: "Yellow—or liver disease— lies ahead, and scarcely more than a year ago, I tried to escape black by suicide."

On the whole, it is less the sequence of ages that holds his attention than the general feeling of a kind of fatality:

> But that is how things happen, how things are done and undone; I am still caught in these Colors of Life, and I have less and less hope of escaping their order (at least by my own will), framed in the wooden oblong like a bad daguerreotype . . .
>
> The endlessly renewed oscillation between "Who am I?" and "What am I?"[1]

The announcements page in the daily newspapers offers a contemporary version of the ages of life, only fragmented and multidimensional. Births, marriages, and deaths share the space there. For each individual named, it is only a matter of one of these rubrics. Each is located in just one of the columns these announcements fill. According to their ages, newspaper readers are more or less apt to be interested in one or another of the rubrics. In this sense, the announcements page is doubly the realm of age. It is a realm to which not everyone has access. You have to pay for the announcements. Only a few privileged individuals benefit from the newspaper's initiative. It is said that a certain national daily newspaper keeps an up-to-date file of individuals whose age and fame guarantee them a choice spot one day in the obituaries. Two dates and a biography, sometimes a few words of praise, will summarize a life. In the realm of age, one tribute follows on the heels of another almost daily. The last sparks of human vanity are thus reduced to a few titles or decorations, a few commendations, perhaps evoking a hint of nervous jealousy among rivals very much alive and awaiting consecration.

The ages-of-life theme can inspire other reflections nonetheless. The ages of life follow one another like the seasons. That is what the expression suggests. The plural invites us, of course, to consider aging as inescapable, but the metaphor of the seasons has special resonances; spring follows winter, we know. Thus it suggests either that a part of the one who dies returns—a theme often the subject of polytheistic and pagan representations—

or that new generations take over from the preceding ones—a theme that can go hand in hand with the first, moreover, and that we will willingly embrace in the idle conversations we sometimes have on this subject. Thus in the plural use of the word "age" there is an element of optimism, in sharp contrast to its use in the singular, which identifies it with an inevitability, a fate with no future. To suggest that generations succeed one another like the seasons is to understand that they share membership in the human race. It is to affirm a humanism of inheritance that can be free from any reference to heredity, provided that it not be limited to the narrow framework of family and biological reproduction.

Between that singular and plural, between "age" and "ages," there is basically an absolute difference and a close complementary relationship. The ages of life can be evoked independently from the progression that advancing age implies, by means of anticipation, which lays out a future, or memory, which recreates the past, and in any case, by letting the imagination play with time.

LOOKING YOUR AGE

"I'd say he wasn't over forty."

Words and common expressions speak volumes, as they say. No doubt they say too much not to contradict themselves, with the confidence of the overly naive or the overly clever. "You don't look your age" is a claim we sometimes hear; it is supposed to please the one to whom it is addressed. Conversely, expressed positively, it is most often used in the third person, in a confidential, pitying tone, referring to an absent third party. She "looks her age," or more insistently, he "really looks his age." The verb in French is not *voir*, to look, but *faire*, to make, and applied to age, it seems misused. Because the one who "makes his age" is subjected to it; he passively suffers the action of time and directly expresses or even anticipates it. One who makes one's age lets him- or herself be made by it. To make one's age is to let it take control. The one who "makes" is passive and submits. On the contrary, the one who does not is presumed to have an active, healthy life, to possess an energy that mitigates or slows the effects of age. I exercise in order not to make—or look—my age. I pull in my belly, I diet, I do thalassotherapy; I try creams and foundations, I use makeup to make myself young, younger, that is to say, than my age.

One does not "take age" as one "takes off" or "takes courage" or "takes his fate into his own hands." More like one "takes cold" or "takes fright." The two principal verbs of action, "to make" and "to take," are ambivalent, and it is enough to change their direct object to shift semantically into the passive voice. This play of passive and active is found again, more clearly, in other expressions with other verbs. One advances in age, as one advances toward someone, but when one arrives, it is the age itself that is said to be "advanced," as if it were a matter of a means of private transport, like when your limousine arrives (*"votre voiture est avancée,"* meaning literally, "your car is advanced" or "your car is here"). When combined, the two expressions nearly collide, as when we say of someone that "he arrived at an advanced age."

"How many years do you give him? Fifty, fifty-five?" By a strange alchemy, the vocabulary here substitutes an offering for an estimate. We often express ourselves this way when, spontaneously and not necessarily falsely, we unconsciously assess the age of our interlocutors. Conversely, we are aware of being continually exposed to the scrutiny of others. "How many do you give him?" It is unclear whether the one at the receiving end would appreciate the contents of the offer, if he knew about it, if, by chance or through the assessor's malice, the estimate was too high. He would wish for less generosity in the attribution of years: "I wouldn't give him more than fifty, I wouldn't take him for his age." That is what an aging man might like to hear. But no one has asked for his opinion. The gift comes unbidden. It is just the echo of a truth imposed by nature and time and that a witness can supposedly discern on the body of another. This witness is only the spokesperson of the irreparable, playing the role of the chorus in Greek tragedy. He only gives to the other what he steals: his image. This false exchange is never so cruel as when it takes the form of an interrogation. "What age would you give me?" an individual too sure of his appearance, out of weakness or imprudence, may sometimes ask the one he believes he has caught unawares and charmed. And the response, if it is accurate, comes as a blow. Yes, he "makes his age," his age is advanced: he has now only to drive away.

This is not a matter of wordplay. Or rather, it is the words that play with us and not the other way around. They confine us to a binary "to be or not to be" system and let us vacillate endlessly between reality and appearance, the natural and the artificial, exposure and disguise, or truth and lie, as if, with regard to age, it was never possible to have the last word.

The uses of language are subtle; they express our doubts, our illusions, and our fears. To desire what one knows one must suffer or simply to accept it: the distinction between heroism and wisdom is minuscule and essential. This dilemma is at the heart of the great moral options of human societies, and it may be useful to rediscover the traces of it scattered throughout the words of the language. Moreover, language evolves, the vocabulary changes, and certain words age; sometimes we even estimate the age of people according to the words they use. In this case, every trick in the book is allowed, and they are often underhanded: one can speak youthfully just as one can dress youthfully. We speak with words, but our words speak of us, even or especially when they lie. Words "make their age," and that is undoubtedly why they speak in such contradictory ways about time.

Of course, with regard to the language of time itself, it is clear that words can easily age overnight. As a primary example, the word *passe-temps*, pastime, is in a bad way: who would dare reduce navigating or "surfing" the Internet to the rank of pastime? Do *jeux de patience*, puzzles, still have a future? Who would dare speak of *l'âge bête*, the age of the beast, to evoke adolescence? Who would dare mention "the woman of thirty" in the Balzacian sense of the term? It is a good bet that the expressions common in my youth will not hold up: soon no one dead or alive will *casser sa pipe*, "break his pipe" (in English, "snuff it"), or *bouffer les pissenlits par la racine*, "push up the daisies." Antitobacco laws, cremation, and defoliants will tidy up the vocabulary. And who these days would *not* want *aller plus vite que la musique* (literally "to go quicker than music") (in English, "run before you walk" or "put the cart before the horse")? Are time and patience still virtues? "Everything comes to those who wait." Belied by experience, for many proverbs, their time has come.

When we say, or think without saying it, that words, expressions, and idioms are "dated," it means that those who use them express or assert a kind of linguistic, social, and historic *retour d'âge*, "return of age" (in English, "change of life") (another expression we no longer use). Whether an effect of age, snobbery, or derision, these language gaps serve as provocation with regard to so-called contemporary language. Thus if someone who is slightly old wants to avoid being considered old-fashioned or anti-establishment, it is to his or her advantage to change vocabulary, to enrich it, certainly, with all the new words that come with the new technologies in use today but also to strip it of outdated words and old-fashioned phrases that are "old hat." Moreover, many people of a certain age devote themselves to this "pastime," often without much trouble and even enthusiastically; if they enjoy it, relations between grandparents and grandchildren play no small part in this regard.

THE AGE OF THINGS AND THE AGE OF OTHERS

"Malraux has aged.
—Less than Gide!"

We sometimes have the feeling that age comes from elsewhere, that it is exterior to us, that things have changed without asking our opinion and that is why we do not recognize them. "This book has aged," we say or sometimes hear said. Or more harshly: "It hasn't aged well." Such remarks are relatively frequent and transform us into unmoving, implacable judges of works and authors. A little reflection leads us quickly to reverse this image: the book's text has not altered, the film's images have not changed. From this perspective, cinema is the inexorable witness of how memory drifts. I have a taste for old movies, especially American ones. There are some I have seen countless times, a benefit of my privilege as a Parisian, such as it is. Parenthetically, I will add that watching a film in a theater is a whole different experience than watching it on DVD or television. It is not immediately reproducible and is never solitary, even in the Latin Quarter theaters that are almost empty during the week. Thus during these visits to the cinema, it is not just a matter of the film; it is also the décor and ritual that have hardly changed. Well, the experience of memory's vagaries remains the same; there is always something more or something less in the actual show than in my memory of it, even when that memory is relatively recent. As soon as it is left to itself, the memory hurries about erasing certain details and adding others—often tiny variations, but enough to demonstrate to me that it is not the film that has changed, much less aged, but me. Film is the irrecusable witness to the memory's astonishing capacity to forget and to invent.

Nevertheless it may be too easy to blame the vagaries of memory and forgetting alone for the apparent aging of the things in life. The things in life belong to three orders: landscapes, works, and beings, or more precisely, bodies. And they are at the source of relationships—relationships that connect us to places, books, relatives, friends, and animals.

Undoubtedly the relationship one has with a landscape is not comparable to the relationship one has with a living being, which assumes a reciprocity. To evoke the supposed permanence of nature in his poem, "The Lake," Lamartine is obliged to personify it:

Oh lake! mute rocks! caves! dark forest!
You whom time spares or that it can rejuvenate,
Retain of this night, beautiful nature, retain at least the
  memory![1]

Which Victor Hugo is very careful not to do when, in
"The Sadness of Olympio," he sees in the changes in the
landscape a confirmation of the irreversible nature of the
past: "Our leafy chambers in the thickets are changed."
It must be said that landscapes are never truly natural
and that their changes are the result of human actions.
If you can no longer find the landscape you have retained
in your memory, it is because you no longer find yourself
there, because it has become a stranger to you (it is very
much a matter of a relationship). But if the landscape
has objectively changed (there's been construction, a forest cleared, a road cut through it), it is because other
humans have intervened. Thus from a certain perspective, it is very much a matter of an intervention into your
personal privacy, and no doubt that is what explains the
virulence of some protests against projects that involve
disrupting the landscape. It is less a matter of ecology
than a kind of attack on private life.

There is still the case of landscapes that are affected by no external interventions but that seem to have
shrunk over time. When Proust returns to Illiers, everything, including the river, seems smaller to him. But how
can we forget that, as children, everything was objectively bigger, beings (the "big people") as well as landscapes?
I have always thought that the miracle of movie theaters

is the size of the figures, immense on the screen, who by their appearance alone restore to us a child's vision, the time when the world of adults was composed of giants twice our size.

As for the rest, the changes we can attribute to time are not necessarily a sign of degradation. When we say that a book or a film "has aged," we are in fact talking about a change in ourselves, of course. But if we pay attention to the fact that there is a relationship (between the book or the film and ourselves) at the starting point of the memory, we must clearly recognize that it is the relationship that has changed and not necessarily the work or us. And that relationship may be enriched; it may have acquired a new energy. Far from indicating a loss of meaning or substance, the change may be positive. I will use as an example two authors who are not at all of equal interest: the Countess of Ségur and Alexandre Dumas.

As a child, my mother had read the Countess of Ségur in the gilt-edged Rose Library edition, and in my bedroom she had left her essential works at my disposal, from *Les malheurs de Sophie* (*Sophie's Misfortunes*) to the *Mémoires d'un âne* (*Memories of a Donkey*) and including *Les petites filles modèles* (*Model Little Girls*) and *Les vacances* (*The Holidays*). From the age of six, I devoured the novels by the Countess, born Sophie Rostopchine, and I must confess that no work ever afterward awakened in me comparable feelings or conjured such potent images. No one will doubt me if I declare that I never reread the Countess of Ségur, not in a donkey's years, as they say, and that I almost reproached my mother, much later, for having put into my hands a literature of class in which good sentiments (acts of charity toward the honest poor) appear side by side with the most reactionary politics (denunciations of the Garibaldi "hordes" advancing on Rome in *Après la pluie le beau temps* [*After the Rain, Blue Skies*]), a spontaneous and almost innocent racism (in the same work, the "Negro" Ramor shows the devotion of a faithful dog toward his master, "Moussu Jacques," and fights at his side in the Papal Zouaves to save the pope and the Vatican), and an uncontrolled tendency toward sexual sadism (there are repeated scenes of whipping naked bottoms, in everything from *Les malheurs de Sophie* to *Général Dourakine* and including *Un bon petit diable* (*A Good Little Devil*). But there remains the fact that the Countess de Ségur had talent; she knew how to awaken the sympathies of young children and appeal to their imaginations. Of course I am sure that her books would not entrance me today if I dared to stick my nose back into them again. Moreover, there would be no point: my memory with regard to the first texts that I read is excellent, whereas it often proves weak when I am searching for more recent references. I believe I have gotten over the vague, unconfessed feelings that the scenes of naked bottoms awakened in me. But long ago, when I happened to be driving down the secondary roads in France at nightfall, I would look for crossroads where the warm, welcoming silhouette of an inn might appear, like the one where the two orphans in *L'auberge de l'ange gardien* (Inn of the

Guardian Angel) might have found refuge. This image with its hazy but insistent outlines has never left me, and it can still lend the fleeting, unfinished air of déjà-vu to countrysides I happen upon at dusk sometimes.

My relationship with the Countess has thus been reduced and magnified, reduced to something less than an image, hardly anything, but it stays with me, and I can sometimes conjure it unexpectedly, almost anywhere, in the recurring form of an unsatisfied desire.

Alexandre Dumas is an author of inexhaustible richness. Every ten or fifteen years I reread *The Three Musketeers*, *Twenty Years After*, *The Vicomte of Bragelonne*, and also *The Count of Monte Cristo*, which are works for which age is the theme and time the subject. I always take pleasure in following the intrigues that develop, and I appreciate more than ever the energy displayed, but it's true that, as time passes, I am more aware of the subtle melancholy that casts a shadow over the sequel to *The Three Musketeers* as each character lives his life and the ties among the four friends loosen, imperceptibly at first, as a result of age and the occupations associated with it. Of course, this vast romantic sequel is a hymn to fidelity. The developments of history, the history of France as Alexandre Dumas imagined and rewrote it, allow his heroes to reaffirm their faithfulness, to keep putting it to the test, and bear witness to it until death. But it is the other side of the story that does not get told, the long years with no more shared adventures, in which age makes itself felt more heavily and in which, without the author's romantic ingenuity, forgetfulness might have consumed everything, or nearly so. *The Count of Monte Cristo* says as much; when his vengeance comes to an end, the Count understands, and is made to feel with cruel courtesy, that for a long time now he has no longer loved Mercédès and that she belongs, as Edmond Dantès himself does, to a vanished past. At the end of the story, we are witnessing something of a footrace between forgetting and the desire for revenge. The threat of forgetting remains hypothetical in *Twenty Years After* and *The Vicomte of Bragelonne*, but its melancholy presence haunts their most beautiful pages. I did not invent it, and it certainly did not wait for me to exist, but twenty or forty years later, I find in *Twenty Years Later* new harmonics that I have had to wait for. We must read and reread; the relationship with a text is alive. A book that does not get old is a book from which the reader can always expect something new, in which he can always discover something, a book that thus demonstrates to him that it is forever alive, that their fates are joined and the two of them are united "for life and till death."

AGING
WITHOUT AGE

I t is in seeing the face again of someone we have
long "lost sight of" that we sometimes become
aware of having aged. Past a certain age, we must never
stray for very long from those whom we are destined to
see again; they will take advantage of that time by aging without warning and reappear suddenly like tact-
less mirrors of our own decrepitude. Among friends with
whom we have stayed in closer contact we may reassure
ourselves: "Age has dealt him quite a blow . . . ," but our
hearts are not in it. We look for an explanation; we wonder if—and we almost wish that—he is ill. And then, if
we become close again (and if he is healthy), we forgive
him, we forget, we rediscover him, we find our way.

We no longer have a simple relationship with our own
bodies, with ourselves. We may not have the chance to
look at ourselves in the mirror every day. When that does

happen, we sometimes avoid contact and withdraw after a quick inexpressive or indifferent glance. But sometimes we linger, either to correct some detail ("to powder one's nose," the expression used to go), fixing makeup, straightening hair or a tie—assuming women still wear makeup, and men, ties—or, just simply, if I may say so, to contemplate the image of ourselves without comment, in an act, literally, of pure reflection. It is the body that we reencounter then, this body that is simultaneously a kind of landscape in its appearance (moreover we like to view it again in photographs more or less "posed," in remembered landscapes, familiar or exotic—the vacation image . . .) and a kind of creation for which we might claim responsibility, like the painter who touches up his painting, as well as a kind of independent being who is living a life that also turns out to be ours. Under such conditions, one's relationship with oneself proceeds through a series of divisions that serve as the occasion for verbal creations: my body and myself (it plays tricks on me or provides me with satisfaction), my consciousness and myself (the stage above, the superego that dominates and represses me, or the stage below with base instincts), me and myself (I am an other). Witness the diversity of an unpredictable self that seems to repeat and reproduce itself exactly but that can also take me by surprise, outstrip and escape me.

Nevertheless, when I look at myself in the mirror and tell myself that I have aged, even though I am interrogating my reflection, referring to it as "you," in that sudden moment of awareness, I am assembling and reunifying my body and my various selves. Returning to the mirror paradoxically releases me from the irresolvable difficulties of reflexive consciousness. I age, therefore I live. I have aged, therefore I am.

It must be said that there is nothing simple about the relationship with oneself, with one's body, and the issue of age only complicates it further.

Traditionally in Africa, the body was considered a surface upon which signs were inscribed beginning from birth, decipherable by specialists, conveying the presence of a hereditary component (the other and the past coexisted there from the beginning), but upon which assaults suffered externally, through disease or various physical mishaps, manifested themselves as well. Here again, specialists were supposed to decipher the source and the meaning of these attacks with the help of a symbolic code that varied from one culture to another but that always existed. Two constants in the symbolic code were nondualism—a systematic nondistinction between body and mind—and a persecutive conception of events, especially of bodily accidents, always considered to be willfully caused by someone. The importance of these persecutive conceptions has often been emphasized, in comparison to the more integrated conceptions of the self associated with modernity.

But in the most modern of societies, the body becomes the object of scrutiny as exacting as in any traditional hereditary African society. In the name of good physical fitness, health, and well-being, there are signs of aging that we track and try to eliminate. At the same time we would like to get rid of all signs that are also those of poverty; thus, in developed countries, obesity is considered a sign of intellectual and economic underdevelopment, now appearing more and more frequently. But even for those who wear themselves out exercising, jogging, or jumping rope their entire lives, even if they watch their diet, in the end, the body will still reveal its age. Thus, if we want to "stay young," it is a matter of learning how to cover up or to lie. Lie to whom? To others and to oneself. To the self as an other. As if there were some other body, some other besides the body.

The most scrutinizing gaze can immediately recognize those tricks that make the skin seem firmer, the neck less wrinkled, or hair less thin. Still the real fight takes place within, and, as in Napoleon's French campaign after Waterloo, it leads from victory to victory until the final defeat. The moment does indeed arrive when the masks fall, when the harsh truth of age spectacularly emerges, a little sooner, a little later, perhaps, but nonetheless inexorably. For a long time, well before the final decline, men gradually renounce their virility, women their femininity, or at least for some, the most flamboyant aspects of their sexual identity. Aging often makes itself felt early, and the physical collapse associated with extreme old age is the outcome of a long history. Both through its external appearance and its internal dysfunctions, the body "betrays" the one who, becoming aware of this collapse, first feels like the body's victim and refuses to admit that this frail shell in the process of dying constitutes his or her whole being and identity.

The "persecutive" consciousness remains alive and well as it turns against those diseases that it personalizes (cancer, the crab) or the faceless fate (age as a harmful power) whose instrument they are.

Two comments in this regard. More or less advanced physical decline is experienced by the one who suffers it—evidence in itself somehow—as a double suffering, physical and mental, inexplicable because it conveys only nature's indifference. It is there, that is all, just as the past is no longer there. But others have experienced this decline much earlier, sometimes as children, and that thought could and ought to temper the bitterness of those who do not want to recognize themselves in the suffering bodies that trap and humiliate them. Visiting hospitals for children and adolescents ought to be recommended to anxious adults. They would understand that, no matter what may happen to them, they will have escaped the worst and, in the moral, persecutive language that is still ours today, the most "unjust" fate.

Awareness of the other, awareness of the fact that the other exists, and not just as possible persecutor: here again is the most effective tool for gaining self-awareness. Because when it is a matter of the other, we have no trouble fully identifying him with his body and the signs produced by it (smiles or tears and their infinite nuances, from enthusiasm to fear), up until the very moment when that body offers no further signs of life and when we must acknowledge that what was no longer is, that the one who existed with all the attributes of life exists no longer.

The illusion that drives us to distinguish ourselves from our bodies, to interrogate, curse, or flatter our bodies, continually comes undone before our eyes. The ruses of reflexive consciousness, the illusion of existing outside and independently of one's own body, fail before the obvious fact of the other's sudden, definitive disappearance when he dies, which introduces a radical break between the before and the after. Out of sight, out of body, there is nothing, there is no longer anything. And the words that humans invented to make themselves believe there was something, first of all the word "death" itself, fraught with terror and hope, only conceal the nothingness.

Solitude is said to be one of the cruelest afflictions of old age. In fact, as time passes the moorings that secure us to the shore come undone or at least slacken. Although some people eagerly anticipate retirement, with a single blow, it imposes a distance from the familiar routine, which can be disconcerting because it so closely resembles a kind of death. It is sometimes celebrated with a ceremony reminiscent of funerals, with speeches, flowers, and sincere feelings.

The problem with the solitude of old age is that it is imposed not only as an obvious personal fact but by way of others, by those who betray, desert, withdraw, founder in disease, or die. You cannot age for long without witnessing many close friends growing distant or disappearing.

The worst of it is that we get used to it. Or we seem to get used to it. As if, not out of indifference but out of decency, we refuse to consider abominable what we know to be the common lot. Also, and at the same time, we grow increasingly indifferent to current events and to others. Léo Ferré has a song about this: "And you feel all alone maybe but easy . . ."

The solitude we suffer, imposed by the death of old companions and the disregard of others; the solitude we desire, as though through a defense mechanism or a form of defiance: are the many types of solitude an inevitable part of old age?

Not necessarily. Whether we "make" it or not, we "have" our age; we have it, but it also has us. For all that, to be old is to be alive, and the signs of age are also the signs of life. Behind the excuses offered by those who prove especially attentive to their bodies, beyond the vanity, we can discern a desire to live fully, as Cicero invites us to do. Living fully is an ideal not available to many over the course of their so-called active lives, because of various constraints that encumber them. Thus sometimes retirement is actually considered to be a kind of liberation and rebirth, an opportunity finally to take time to live—to live without counting, to take one's time without further concerns about age.

A question of luck, on the one hand: some are less affected than others by the afflictions of age, or affected later. As a result, they spontaneously acquire the wisdom of the cat and ask the body only to give what it can. They identify with it and shrewdly save their strength. Thus they constitute an example we can oppose to all the pessimistic reports on the disaster of old age. We may sometimes be surprised by the unaffected good humor of some old people who seem to have waited until the end to learn to enjoy life, thus epitomizing in some way the saying often quoted as the classic example of stating the obvious: "Five minutes before his death, Monsieur de La Palisse was still alive." Yes, exactly.

NOSTALGIA

What remains of our love,
What remains of those beautiful days?
—TRENET

There are two kinds of nostalgia: one that focuses on the past that we lived and one that
focuses on the past that we might have lived. The first is
conjugated in the present conditional ("I would love to
return to those happy days"); the second is conjugated in
the past conditional ("If I had dared to act, I would have
succeeded"). Taking over for and nurtured by a more or
less faithful memory, the first runs head-on into the ir-
reversibility of time. The second does not just want to return to the past but to change history ("If I had listened
to my parents . . . , if I hadn't let myself be convinced . . . ,
if I had left . . . , if I had stayed . . . , life might have been

different"). Linguistically, it is conjugated in the unreal past mood, that is, from the perspective of the present, a kind of double unreal since, in substituting reproach for regret, it focuses not on what was and will not return but on what never was and might have been.

We sometimes express the symmetrical, reverse idea when we think about small events—chance encounters, sudden impulses, various strokes of luck—that have shaped our existence and might never have happened: "If I had arrived five minutes later, if I hadn't delayed leaving for vacation, my life might not have taken the turn it did."

Nostalgia or the height of bad faith: when its target is time, it performs a ruthless selection; forgetfulness is its secret and particularly effective weapon, a sharp knife that cuts ever deeper into the layers of memory and invents a past that never existed. In our heart of hearts, we know perfectly well that all was not paradise at the time of our earliest loves; what we wish for, even in knowing the vanity of this wish, is to return there now with our emptiness, our desires, and our imagination. What we miss never existed since it is, on the contrary, our present projection, the projection of our present desire, that gives it its existence. In the end, the two kinds of nostalgia merge, and the second, which surely gives rise to the most painful states of mind, at least has the merit of a certain lucidity, not when it calls up what might have been but because it acknowledges the failings and deficiencies that marked the past as we actually experienced it.

In both cases, nostalgia says much about our present and delights in playing with time, which explains its ambivalence. Because if it can express regrets, it is often the occasion for true pleasure, analogous no doubt to the pleasure of writers who invent the imaginary pasts of their heroes by borrowing from their own memories and imagination. With regard to our pasts, we are all creators and artists. We advance facing backward, forever observing and reconstructing the times gone by. Thus the proverb proves false: old age knows no better than youth. Age knows that ignorance has no bearing on timidity. What old people recognize is that they already knew and they did not dare. That is very much the basis for the second kind of nostalgia.

The refrains of popular songs, which we do not necessarily consider masterpieces but cheerfully hum along with when we hear a street musician torture them in the Métro or outside a café, do not call up the past as much as a form of permanence for us. This is the permanence of desires laid to rest that, with just a few notes, will spring back to life in a moment, intact and as vain and troubling as they ever were.

Conscious illusion, the pleasure of a vague melancholy that is not limited to emotional memories or feelings of love but reawakens deep within us, for a moment, the awareness of some lack. Among older people, it does not manifest itself in dreams of the future or projects, as it did in their youth—although some youths are too sensible and some old people a bit wild—but it is still very much the same awareness. A happy consciousness of some beneficial incompletion that fosters the desire for creation, the desire for something or somewhere else, the preeminent sign of life, where past and future mix, sign of the time that passes and returns like a song's refrain, sign without age.

Nostalgia is a powerful, and therefore potentially dangerous, force. It can fuel the most insane and most reactionary passions. Today we find some "nostalgia" for the Third Reich among young men whose image of it obviously comes from others. A past one has not known is the easiest kind to claim and reconstruct. In a more general way, political nostalgia marks a third category that is as distinct from nostalgia that focuses on the past as it is from nostalgia that focuses on a past that might have been. Traditionalists and reactionaries are combatants of the imaginary, utopians devoted to a past as illusory as the utopia of progressives, but those of the former category are more hypocritical, founding the new order to which they aspire on a nonexistent or shameful past. On a wider scale, political life takes ambiguous recourse in a reconstructed past that plays or tries to play on the evocation of times gone by, great examples, and great men, in order to suggest that anything could become possible again. Everything lies in the prefix "re-," which seems to postulate the existence of an actual history that we would only have to rediscover, as if today's virtual reality were yesterday's actual reality. Thus our mythic dates are born, with their mythic power varying according to political sensibilities, and in any case, with a symbolic force that exceeds objective content: 1936, 1945, May '68 . . .

None of these dates leaves me indifferent. Like everyone, I associate the first with cinematographic images of workers taking their first paid vacations; I experienced the elation of the Liberation, and then Victory; as for many, my life was never completely the same after 1968. Still it remains true that if we stick to actual history, in each case it is certainly more complex than the image associated with the date. And regarding the symbolic power of the date, the more brightly it shines the more it is used, especially if it is abused, especially with regard to younger generations.

The past's influence on individual lives goes by many names. "Nostalgia" is one of them. "Routine" is another. Routine is habit without interruption, a continuity that does not feel compelled to think about itself, an unconscious fidelity, an idleness. Nostalgia comes to undermine the routine, possibly to test it by reintroducing the idea of the possible into the humdrum daily rounds, otherwise free of problems and questions.

Encountering the other—love, including passionate love—is above all an opportunity to experience intensely our solitude and the "desert" that surrounds us. That is the melancholic, almost desperate theme of authors like the Japanese novelist Haruki Murakami (*South of the Border, West of the Sun*). Shimamoto-san is the chaste adolescent lover of the hero, about whom he never stops dreaming, reliving through memory the scenes of their emotional and intellectual intimacy. When life separated them, he was not able or never dared to remedy the situation (the two kinds of nostalgia at work in him). After many years of absence, she reappears suddenly as a mysterious woman, then disappears again after one night of love. He has learned nothing about her present life, and he thus finds himself alone again with his wife Yukiko and realizes that he has never really spoken to her ("It's true, I never asked her anything"). One never learns anything ("I seemed to have again become the adolescent I was, powerless and lost"). Except, perhaps, for lack of knowing who one is, to try to learn to come out of oneself: "No one will weave dreams for me—it is my turn to weave dreams for others. That's what I have to do now."

Thus, leaving nostalgia behind may be a way of finding the other again in order to rediscover oneself. A difficult task, unless, as some pages of the novel suggest, the hero had already decided to trade in one nostalgia for another, after having been foolish enough to subject the first one to the test of an actual return.

Clearly it is not easy to switch nostalgias as we like. Nevertheless, we all have images that linger in our minds and surface unexpectedly from time to time, by chance, and without reason. They do not necessarily correspond to significant events; we may not be able to date them precisely. They are simply there. These are not obsessions; they are discreet and will desist if we show no interest in retaining them. But they return at one time or another as if to assure us that they remain available: fragments of landscape, glimpsed faces, roadsides, seasides . . . Even when there is an anecdote to support them, they escape it; they are less precise but more faithful. Some emerge from a distant and almost forgotten childhood. Rather than trying desperately to find their meaning in the mysteries of the psyche, to wonder what they are concealing, perhaps we could recognize them as signs of the times that do not want to die, links between a lost past and an unknown future, spare nostalgias, ready for use.

EVERYONE DIES YOUNG

I have had many cats in my life, female cats most often, that, after a first and only experience, surgery quickly denied the pleasures of mating and the feelings of reproduction. With each of them, it was the same story beginning over again: the mischievousness of the first months, triumphant maturity, gradual loss of powers, and always the same serenity. The ages of life paraded past at an accelerated pace. One of the virtues of pets, from the human perspective, is surely their ability to replace one another. Their quick succession dispenses with the work of grieving, and when a person of a certain age decides not to replace the last one to die, it may be because this time, their fates risk being parallel.

The death of a last cat or dog that will not be replaced, whether because of material circumstances or weariness, in any case marks a change in point of view.

Until then, the animal existed, from our perspective, as a mortal in the presence of immortals. We may regard dogs and cats with the same gaze as the Homeric gods cast upon humans: with sympathy but also with the sad awareness of being able to do nothing to change their fate. But we are not immortals, hardly even demigods, when it comes to our animals. Deciding not to replace the last one to die is admitting that, like our animals, we are mortal. It is a way of identifying with them. It is also an opportunity for us to ponder the secret of their serenity, their closeness to nature, what Bataille called "intimacy," suggesting that ultimately it is incompatible with individuality. In fact, it is at the age when we become most acutely aware of the proximity of the moment when our individuality will dissolve, that we become the most sensitive to what, in the wisdom of the cat, seems to have long anticipated that event.

The problem with humans, nevertheless, is that there are individual human consciousnesses that need others in order to exist fully. Rousseau must recognize that the happy moments he experienced on the shores of Lake Bienne were not attributable solely to his merging with the surrounding natural world but also to the friendly presence of his hosts. Friendship, love, and grief are signs of life linked to the presence of others. Aging allows us to explore other encounters and relationships—or sometimes requires us to suffer them. It is an experience that becomes ever more diverse as life expectancy increases, as we can see in the guileless, now commonplace euphemisms, the third and fourth age.

But one's awareness of self does not always follow suit. If I have a hard time bending down to pick up the key that I dropped, for the image I retain of myself, this gesture still takes no effort. I protest if I am offered help—a little more gently, it is true, as my stiffness increases. After all, is it so contrary to exercise in order to retain a little flexibility and to avoid the embarrassment of having to ask for help with bags on the train? To age is to try out new human relationships; it is a privilege that many will never know, which is a good thing to be aware of. It is also the opportunity for some to experience what they had only imagined in wondering what their elders felt, rejoining them in one sense and thus lessening the distance between generations. Old age may know something after all: that it is nothing to make a fuss over, as they said when I was a child. Old age is like exoticism: others viewed from a distance by the ignorant. Old age does not exist.

Time, as old age experiences it, is not the accumulated, ordered sum of the events of the past. It is a palimpsest; everything inscribed there does not reappear, and sometimes the earliest inscriptions surface most easily. Alzheimer's disease is only an acceleration of the natural selection process of forgetting, at the end of which it seems that the most tenacious—if not the most faithful—images are often those of childhood. Whether we delight in this fact or deplore it, because there is a share of cruelty in such an observation, we must nevertheless admit it: everyone dies young.

NOTES

THE WISDOM OF THE CAT

1. Manon Gauthier-Faure, *Le Monde* (August 9, 2013).

AS AGE APPROACHES

1. Cicero, *Cato the Elder, or On Old Age*, trans. W. A. Falconer, Loeb Classical Library (Cambridge, Mass.: Harvard University Press, 1923), 7:22.

HOW OLD ARE YOU?

1. Definition of age by the French National Institute of Statistics and Economic Studies (INSEE).
2. Charles Baudelaire, "Spleen (II)," in *The Flowers of Evil (Les fleurs du mal)*, trans. Richard Howard (Boston: David R. Godine, 1982).

1. Michel Leiris, *L'âge d'homme* (Paris: Gallimard, 1973). English edition: *Manhood: A Journey from Childhood Into the Fierce Order of Virility*, trans. Richard Howard (Chicago: University of Chicago Press, 1992).

2. Walter Benjamin, *Gesammelte Briefe, Band VI: 1938–1940* (Berlin: Suhrkamp, 2000). Letter to Max Horkheimer, March 23, 1940, in "Georges Bataille: D'un monde l'autre," *Critique* 788–789 (January–February 2013): 106.

3. Stefan Zweig, *Le monde d'hier. Souvenirs d'un Européen* (Paris: Le Livre de Poche, 1996). English edition: *The World of Yesterday*, trans. Anthea Bell (Lincoln: University of Nebraska Press, 2013).

4. Simone de Beauvoir, "Prologue," *La force de l'âge* (Paris: Gallimard, 1986). English edition: *The Prime of Life*, trans. Peter Green (World Publishing, 1962).

5. Gustave Flaubert, *L'éducation sentimentale* (Paris: Gallimard, 2005). English edition: *Sentimental Education; or, The Story of a Young Man*, trans. Dora Knowlton Ranous (Bretano's, 1922).

6. Jean-Jacques Rousseau, *Les rêveries du promeneur solitaire*, "Cinquième promenade" (1776–1778). English edition: *Reveries of the Solitary Walker* (J. Bew, 1783).

CLASS

1. Denise Paulme, ed., *Classes et associations d'âge en Afrique de l'Ouest* (Paris: Plon, 1971).

IMAGES D'ÉPINAL

1. Michel Leiris, *L'âge d'homme* (Paris: Gallimard, 1973). English edition: *Manhood: A Journey from Childhood Into the Fierce Order of Virility*, trans. Richard Howard, trans. (Chicago: University of Chicago Press, 1992).

THE AGE OF THINGS
AND THE AGE OF OTHERS

1. Alphonse de Lamartine, "Le lac," *Méditations poétique* (1820).

INDEX

European Perspectives
A Series in Social Thought and Cultural Criticism
LAWRENCE D. KRITZMAN, EDITOR

Pierre Vidal-Naquet, *The Jews: History, Memory, and the Present*

Karl Löwith, *Martin Heidegger and European Nihilism*

Pierre Nora, *Realms of Memory: The Construction of the French Past*

Vol. 1: *Conflicts and Divisions*

Vol. 2: *Traditions*

Vol. 3: *Symbols*

Alain Corbin, *Village Bells: Sound and Meaning in the Nineteenth-Century French Countryside*

Louis Althusser, *Writings on Psychoanalysis: Freud and Lacan*

Claudine Fabre-Vassas, *The Singular Beast: Jews, Christians, and the Pig*

Tahar Ben Jelloun, *French Hospitality: Racism and North African Immigrants*

Alain Finkielkraut, *In the Name of Humanity: Reflections on the Twentieth Century*

Emmanuel Levinas, *Entre Nous: Essays on Thinking-of-the-Other*

Zygmunt Bauman, *Globalization: The Human Consequences*

Emmanuel Levinas, *Alterity and Transcendence*

Alain Corbin, *The Life of an Unknown: The Rediscovered World of a Clog Maker in Nineteenth-Century France*

Carlo Ginzburg, *Wooden Eyes: Nine Reflections on Distance*

Sylviane Agacinski, *Parity of the Sexes*

Michel Pastoureau, *The Devil's Cloth: A History of Stripes and Striped Fabric*

Alain Cabantous, *Blasphemy: Impious Speech in the West from the Seventeenth to the Nineteenth Century*

Julia Kristeva, *The Sense and Non-Sense of Revolt: The Powers and Limits of Psychoanalysis*

Kelly Oliver, *The Portable Kristeva*

Gilles Deleuze, *Dialogues II*

Catherine Clément and Julia Kristeva, *The Feminine and the Sacred*

Sylviane Agacinski, *Time Passing: Modernity and Nostalgia*

Luce Irigaray, *Between East and West: From Singularity to Community*

Julia Kristeva, *Hannah Arendt*

Julia Kristeva, *Intimate Revolt: The Powers and Limits
of Psychoanalysis*, vol. 2

Elisabeth Roudinesco, *Why Psychoanalysis?*

Régis Debray, *Transmitting Culture*

Steve Redhead, ed., *The Paul Virilio Reader*

Claudia Benthien, *Skin: On the Cultural Border Between Self
and the World*

Julia Kristeva, *Melanie Klein*

Roland Barthes, *The Neutral: Lecture Course at the Collège de France
(1977–1978)*

Hélène Cixous, *Portrait of Jacques Derrida as a Young Jewish Saint*

Theodor W. Adorno, *Critical Models: Interventions and Catchwords*

Julia Kristeva, *Colette*

Gianni Vattimo, *Dialogue with Nietzsche*

Emmanuel Todd, *After the Empire: The Breakdown
of the American Order*

Gianni Vattimo, *Nihilism and Emancipation: Ethics, Politics, and Law*

Hélène Cixous, *Dream I Tell You*

Steve Redhead, *The Jean Baudrillard Reader*

Jean Starobinski, *Enchantment: The Seductress in Opera*

Jacques Derrida, *Geneses, Genealogies, Genres, and Genius: The Secrets
of the Archive*

Hélène Cixous, *White Ink: Interviews on Sex, Text, and Politics*

Marta Segarra, ed., *The Portable Cixous*

François Dosse, *Gilles Deleuze and Félix Guattari: Intersecting Lives*

Julia Kristeva, *This Incredible Need to Believe*

François Noudelmann, *The Philosopher's Touch: Sartre, Nietzsche, and
Barthes at the Piano*

Antoine de Baecque, *Camera Historica: The Century in Cinema*

Julia Kristeva, *Hatred and Forgiveness*

Roland Barthes, *How to Live Together: Novelistic Simulations of Some
Everyday Spaces*

Jean-Louis Flandrin and Massimo Montanari, *Food:
A Culinary History*